Dan Young and Star Group International
have made this gift edition available
in honor of
Northwood University's 40th Anniversary
and its founder,
Dr. Arthur E. Turner.

101 Reasons to READ to Your Child

101 Reasons to READ to Your Child

Brenda Star

First Edition

STARGROUP
INTERNATIONAL INC

Star Group International, Inc. Book Division
West Palm Beach, Florida

Published 2000

FIRST EDITION

Designed and produced by Star Group International, Inc.

Printed in the United States of America

Library of Congress Card Number: 99-69040

101 Reasons to READ to Your Child
ISBN I-884886-10-8

This book is available for quantity purchases, sales promotions, premiums, fundraising or educational use. For more information contact:
Star Group International
777 S. Flagler Drive, West Tower, Eighth Floor
West Palm Beach, FL 33401
(561) 547-0667

Dedication

To the parents, teachers and individuals who choose to accept this challenge to make a difference.

Table of Contents

Preface

Recently, while on vacation, I experienced a vision problem. Although not able to read, I was able to watch television. I watched more television that week than I ever had in my entire life. I realized during that time, that children today are being exposed to an enormous amount of violence and degradation via the television, rather than discovering the incredible world of reading.

I shared this realization with two friends who are long-time school teachers. We discussed the happy times and memories surrounding time that we spent reading to our children when they were young. They immediately started throwing out some very impressive facts about reading. After further research on the topic... I had a mission! I had to share this information with parents and grandparents in a book, *101 Reasons to Read to Your Child*. I hope these thoughts will bring about some positive changes in the lives of families and their children.

Special Thanks

To Barbara Schuster and Linda Bruno for helping me become aware of the problems and statistics surrounding literacy in this country.

To my two wonderful daughters who gave me the opportunity to practice these ideas and who continue to be a testimony to these reasons to read.

To the numerous dedicated educators who offered suggestions: Lynn Slusher, Carolyn Tye, Ann Garrett, Mary Helen Sakell Arios, and to the Star Group team who helped orchestrate this project, especially Rick Dandes, Mel Abfier, Tom Provost, Veronica Kraft, Diane Roccisano, Arthur Abravanel and Breck Bachle.

Introduction

In many homes the ability to communicate with each other has been lost. We often live as mere strangers under the same roof, passing as ships in the night.

Whatever happened to the kind of families that populated old-time TV-hits like *The Donna Reed Show* or *Father Knows Best*? Where is the family harmony oozing from the Huxstables? The problem is, TV only reflects the values of the times, and the times have changed.

Let's not ignore values that should be preserved. What about family unity and communication? What about gathering our family's support when we need it? What about taking responsibility for our childrens' futures by being positive role models to them? These are endearing qualities and universal values. Modern life runs in high gear, yet a family unit can redefine itself in today's terms and not lose the emotional foundations that keep it healthy.

How can this be done?

By reading to our children.

A half-hour of reading daily can reshape and improve the quality of family life between parent and child. It can be the haven of peace in a hectic day. Reading can unite family members of all ages.

Turn the page to find out why and how...

Facts

- One of the best predictors of whether a child will function competently in school and go on to contribute actively to society is the level to which the child progresses in reading.
  —*National Association for the Education of Young Children*

- According to the National Commission on Reading, there is "no more important activity for preparing your child to succeed as a reader than reading aloud together." At just a few months of age, an infant can look at pictures, listen to your voice and point to pictures on pages. By drawing attention to pictures and associating the words with pictures and objects, children learn the importance of language.

- At all grade levels, students who reported talking about their reading activities with family or friends once or twice a week, or at least monthly, had higher average reading scores than students who reported doing so rarely or never.
  —*from a recent National Assessment of Educational Progress (NAEP) survey on reading*

- Academic success, as defined by high school graduation, can be predicted with reasonable accuracy by knowing someone's reading skill at the end of grade three. A person who is not at least a modestly skilled reader by the end of third grade is quite unlikely to graduate from high school.

  —*National Research Council*

- The U.S. Department of Education's Commission of Reading, after evaluating 10,000 research findings, issued a 1985 report called "Becoming a Nation of Readers," which found "the single most important activity for building the knowledge required for eventual success is reading aloud to children." Furthermore, it claimed that it is necessary for adults to read aloud to children throughout all the grades.

- As the child's first teacher, parents have a significant role in influencing achievement and attitudes about school. When one considers that, from birth to age 18, a child spends approximately 12 percent of his or her life in school, the need to promote a productive learning environment in the home becomes very significant. Parents can create a curriculum at home that teaches children skills and the importance of schools.
  —Source, U. S. Department of Education, 1986

- Schools should promote independent reading outside of school by such means as daily at-home reading assignments and expectations, summer reading lists, encouraging parental involvement. . .
  —Starting Out Right: A Guide to Promoting Children's Reading Success," National Academy of Sciences, 1998

- By the time children enter school, they have had numerous family literacy-learning experiences. Studies show that the extent of these learning experiences, their nature and how they relate to school literacy are of great importance for children's later academics.

  —The International Reading Association

- "Only half of infants and toddlers are routinely read to by their parents, and many parents do not engage in other activities to stimulate their child's intellectual development. It is not surprising then, that teachers report that 35 percent of American kindergarten children arrive at school unprepared to learn."

  —Carnegie Foundation report, as quoted in
  The Read Aloud Handbook, by Jim Trelease

- A child who reads 33.4 minutes a day... magazines, books and newspapers... will be exposed to 2,357,000 words a year. That's an average of about 6,457 words per day. That child also scores in the 90th percentile rank in achievement.

  —Reading Research Quarterly, vol. 3, 1988

- According to the National Institute for Literacy, 7 in 10 prisoners performed in the lower 2 literacy levels.

- *A recent U.S. Department of Education study of almost 25,000 eighth graders found that students watched television an average of 21.2 hours a week, but spent a mere 1.9 hours a week reading.*

And now...
101 Reasons
to
READ
to Your Child

1 Encourages Bonding

Bonding is the ability to trust one another implicitly. Intimate contact while reading with your family can become the basis for this trust. Bonding on a daily basis makes the private time with our children a source of comfort. When they have doubts and questions, they will know we are there for them.

Bridges the Generation Gap 2

Reading together gives us the opportunity to extend ourselves and our love to our children. During difficult times it can draw us together. Shared reading time is a great time to discuss issues with our children. Whether or not we agree with them, reading helps us find a way to solve problems and deal with issues together, as a family.

3 Encourages Character Development

One way to teach character development is through exposure to good characters from great books.

Explains the Meaning of Success 4

Commitment, goals and hard work... these concepts become understandable to children of all ages when they read stories about the success of others.

5 Builds Self-Confidence

We feel good about ourselves and our family ties when we spend time reading together.

Teaches Responsibility 6

The concept of "taking responsibility" is one that needs to be strengthened by parental advice during our children's formative years. Reading helps prepare our children to learn how to accept their own responsibility. It also helps prevent them from accepting any burden that isn't theirs.

7 Increases Sense of Worthiness

Encouraging our children to select reading materials strengthens their sense of self-worth, good judgment and independence.

Shows Family Support 8

Family roles are redefined and strengthened by the simple acts we do as a family unit. By reading aloud to our children, we show that we support them as they are learning how to read.

9 Encourages Self-Expression

Exposure to reading enables children to better express their thoughts and ideas.

Develops Integrity 10

Reading can help develop a child's values and morality through exposure to good and bad characters, situations and their outcomes.

11 Promotes Self-Respect

Nothing shows respect more than talking *with* your child, rather than *to* your child. Instead of being just an authority figure, spending time reading with your children shows respect for them as developing human beings. Respect is the foundation of self-worth.

Fosters Independence 12

While reading together, even the youngest child will begin to feel independent because they are interacting as equals with grownups. Our children feel empowered by being a valuable part of the family experience. Independence is one of the greatest attributes a child can develop.

13 Instills a Sense of Mutual Respect (Parent for Child; Child for Parent)

Reading time strengthens the idea that our life experiences merit respect and that our roles as parents are vital to our children's well-being. Similarly, we learn to respect one another's choices.

Teaches Your Child How to Ask for Help 14

Interacting with your child while reading to him will naturally lead to questions. This exercise teaches children how to ask for help, and how to give help.

15 Helps You to Better Understand Your Child

Sharing reading choices among family members can be a great way to involve yourself and understand your child's point-of-view.

Shares Adult Point-of-View with Child 16

Alternating reading choices can be a great way to share what you like to read...and leads to discussions about your viewpoints.

17 Explains How Reading can be Instructional

No doubt, reading can be a joy, but it is also a necessity when following instructions. For example: when following recipes, manuals, food labels or directions.

Becomes an Educational Tool 18

In order to complete schooling, we must be able to read text books, manuals, guides... and understand them.

19 Helps Raise Academic and Social Performance

Being informed of our children's academic strengths and weaknesses through our reading time, helps us understand what is going on in their lives.

Looks at World History in Exciting New Ways 20

Books document history... and history is full of lessons to be learned. By reading, our children can learn from the past.

21 Helps with Habits and Attitudes

Parents can help their children learn to read for the sheer pleasure of reading. Once good reading habits are established, the child will then be receptive to reading more complex books, and books with differing viewpoints.

Identifies Interests and Nurtures Them 22

We identify, reinforce and expand our children's interests through the selection of the books we read together.

23 Teaches Spirituality Through Examples

Some stories teach us how to have a loving attitude toward family, friends, strangers and our environment. To many, this is the essence of spirituality.

Creates a Family Culture 24

Culture is an important aspect of family life and is passed down through generations. Our family interactions are the lessons of our culture and create lasting values. By reading with our children, they in turn, will become cultural teachers during their own lives.

25   Creates Warm Family Memories

The time you and your children share together now will be remembered for the rest of your lives.

Teaches How to Express Ideas   26

Through reading books, children learn how words are put together to form ideas and stories.

27   Encourages a Variety of Reading Materials

Not all reading has to be school-related. Older children can be read to from newspapers, magazines and books. By reading to them from a variety of sources, they are then encouraged to read from different reading materials when on their own.

Nurtures You (as the Reader) 28

Reading with your child is a loving act. You grow as an individual by giving your time to your child.

29 Redefines Parenthood; Expanding the Parental Role

When we share the reading experience, parents learn that authority is best based on mutual understanding and respect.

Builds Special One-on-One Relationships 30

Especially in large families, reading aloud to a child is a good way to establish a close one-on-one relationship.

31 Allows You to Become an Intellectual Role Model

When we read to our children, we become their intellectual role models. This encourages our children to become role models for their children.

Allows for Better Understanding of Each Other 32

Our children never outgrow the need for our understanding and love. We must find appropriate ways to show it as they mature. Reading together is one way to show our understanding and love for our children.

33 Develops Critical Thinking

Through exposure to books with different points of view, children begin to develop the ability to make carefully considered choices. This is an important step toward critical thinking.

Expands Knowledge and an Appreciation for the Arts 34

Parents can introduce their children to the fine arts through books. It can be beneficial to all children to love and appreciate the arts as part of life.

35 Promotes Healthy Problem Solving

Togetherness promotes the sharing of problems before someone explodes in anger or discontent. Through reading, problems can be explored and resolved.

Helps Face Fears of the Unknown 36

By making the unknown familiar... like going to the dentist for the first time, or facing an operation... there is less fear. Reading helps us face our fears of the unknown.

37 Can Ease a Child's Fears When a New Baby Joins the Family

Reading related books on the subject can help with the child's fears about how he will be treated and what to expect when a new baby comes home.

Reduces Overall Family Tension 38

Reading aloud together is a social interaction. If there is tension in the family, social interaction can help make the situation better. Reading a good book can also lead to conversations that relieve tension.

39 Teaches that Individual Differences are Okay

Dealing effectively with differing points-of-view is something that can be learned during the give-and-take of reading discussions.

Creates New Family Ties 40

Family unity can be created from the communication and closeness that results from reading together.

41 Strengthens Old Family Ties

By reading to our children, we help them understand that they are part of a family unit that grows as the family grows.

Curbs Inappropriate Emotions 42

By letting our children interact with us, we let them know they are being heard and that there is no reason to withdraw or overreact.

43 Teaches How to Share Emotional Space

Setting aside time to read to our children creates an emotional space for us to share feelings and thoughts.

Explains Difficult Situations 44

Through reading, we can find new ways to explain difficult concepts such as divorce, illness or death, in ways that don't over-whelm our children.

45 Examines Unfamiliar Ideas

Improving a child's reading skills can allow him or her to explore other possibilities and take his or her imagination to distant corners of the world.

Establishes a Family Activity 46

Reading to your child establishes a positive routine for today's on-the-run family. Activities done in concert with reading... drawing pictures, locating places on a map, make reading more interesting.

47 Encourages Laughing Together

Laughing together can lighten our burdens. Humorous books are a welcome break from our hectic daily lives.

Encourages A Sense of Wonder 48

We should always encourage the child-like qualities of openness and curiosity. Questions like, "Why do the stars fall?" or "Where does the moon go during the day?" should always be encouraged.

49 Shares Wisdom

By expanding our reading list to include the great visionaries of our time, such as Amelia Earhart, Martin Luther King, Jr. and Frank Lloyd Wright, we can share the wealth of information man has gained throughout the years.

Helps Them Imagine Their "Impossible" Careers 50

As our children learn about career choices, we encourage them to dream their impossible dreams through reading about them. After all, who can say what kind of jobs will exist in outer space?

51

Teaches Family History

Reading books about family events or family history can help our children understand their own family history.

Teaches How Career Choices are Made

52

Exploring career choices through reading allows children to see a variety of roles, situations and possibilities for themselves.

53

Increases Quality Time Together

There is nothing old-fashioned about sitting close to our children and enjoying quality time together.

Teaches Teamwork 54

Reading together and solving problems gives our children an early start in developing the skills of teamwork, which is the first indicator of success in school.

55 Develops the Ability to Read Alone

By reading to your child, you teach your child the skills necessary to read alone. The more you read to them and demonstrate your love of reading, the more likely they'll become avid readers themselves.

Helps Develop Decision-Making Skills 56

We all need to see the "What ifs" in life, and that there are no decisions without consequences. Reading *Aesop's Fables* is a good example of aiding decision-making skills.

57 Helps Understand Cultural Differences

Reading opens up a whole world of experiences. Even if we never venture from our own hometown or country, we can visit any place in the world we desire, by reading about it.

Teaches How to Focus 58

A fundamental skill of learning is how to focus. Shared reading time is all about focusing on the story being read, and listening for important information. Learning to focus on important information helps our children focus in everyday life.

59   Improves Homework

Positive interaction from shared reading time can help ease the difficulties that may arise with homework. By sharing reading time, we enable our children to openly ask questions. This can help improve their results on homework and on exams.

Creates a Work Ethic   60

By expressing our expectations for achievement and responding to our child's reading initiatives and interests, we can create a "positive work ethic."

61   Improves Writing Skills

Proficient readers usually become good writers. Reading encourages self-expression, which enhances one's writing skills.

Improves Performance in School 62

Learning should be a lifelong activity first modeled at home. Studies indicate that success in school can be predicted by a child's third-grade reading scores on achievement tests.

63 Increases Vocabulary Through Exposure to New Words

Children understand several hundred words when they first start school, but they may only be able to read a few dozen. By reading books to your children, you introduce them to an entire world of new words.

Exposes Listener to Good Grammar 64

The more a child is exposed to the written word and grammatically correct sentences, the more likely he or she will use words correctly in the future.

65 Trains the Child in Proper Pronunciation (and Phonics)

Besides expanding a child's vocabulary, reading aloud teaches the proper pronunciation of words.

Stretches the Attention Span and Memory 66

By asking your child to describe what was just read, we are training the mind to remember things.

67 Encourages Curiosity

By reading to our children, we can become a major contributor to their sense of wonder. A child's curiosity is sparked by what is heard, seen and experienced.

Enhances Listening Skills 68

Parents can direct their children's attention when it starts to wander by reading aloud to them and by asking them to repeat what was just read.

69 Encourages Literacy

Literacy is the ability to understand the value of language and its written forms. We are encouraging literacy every time we share reading time with our children.

Encourages Educated Speech 70

Exposure to language that is vastly different from normal television fare can put the child on the path to educated speech. Hollywood's version of speech isn't necessarily grammatically correct.

71 Gives Pre-schoolers a Head Start

Reading to our children, even before they can read themselves, gives them a head start when they begin school. Begin reading nursery rhymes, Mother Goose stories and poems.

Encourages Self-Expression 72

Encouraging children to participate in a shared reading experience improves an important personal skill: the ability to independently express thoughts.

73 Teaches Children to be Nurturing Parents

Reading aloud to your children is nurturing. Nurturing your child sets an example of how your children should nurture their own children in the future.

Teaches How to Learn from Mistakes 74

Children who make mistakes need to understand that they are still loved although they have made a mistake. This helps them learn how to discuss their mistakes with their parents, teachers and peers.

75 Introduces the Child to the Richly Textured Lives of Different People

Books introduce children to the lives of people far beyond their comprehension: for example, the lives of the rich and famous; or the lives of people who live on rice farms in Asia .

Stimulates the Imagination 76

Reading stimulates the imagination and encourages children to create scenes and visions in their minds. Through reading, children have the opportunity to travel in their minds to any corner of the world.

77 Creates Intellectual Challenges

When we read to our children, we challenge them to understand new concepts, which encourages questions and critical thinking.

Stimulates a World View of Ethnic Diversity 78

Reading books about foreign lands expands a child's understanding of differences in people throughout the world.

79 Exposes a Child to Current Affairs

Reading newspapers and magazines exposes a child to news at home and around the world.

Develops an Appreciation of the Written Word 80

By actually reading themselves or encouraging their children to read, parents and children can develop an appreciation for the written word.

81 Creates a Sense of Belonging

Children should feel like a vital part of the family. Spending time reading to our children helps them understand and accept the difficulties of development. Feeling accepted gives them the insight to create healthier circles of friends, work companions and mates.

82 Helps the Child Distinguish Between Fact and Fiction

At a very young age, children have a hard time realizing that characters in story books are not real. With shared reading time, we can begin the process of teaching our children the difference between fact and fiction.

Increases Awareness of the Real World 83

Reading about real-world situations makes children more aware of life's challenges and successes. It also helps them to hold on to their visions of what the world could be, and gives them the ability to work through the reality of the present and the promise of the future. Through reading, they can see their place in the world and their possibilities for success.

84   Improves Infant Motor Skills

Reading to toddlers from a story-board book improves their dexterity and concentration by letting them turn the pages for you.

Can Help Build Long-Distance Relationships   85

Particularly for absentee parents or grandparents, reading to or with a child at a predetermined time over the phone can build a long-distance relationship.

86   Instills a Love of Books

Through our enthusiasm to read, a child can develop a love for books and a passion to read.

Can Calm or Help a Child Go to Sleep   *87*

Babies love to listen to the human voice. Bedtime story-reading can send your young child into dreamland, or it can simply calm him or her down.

88   Makes Vacations More Memorable By Knowing About Where You Are Going

Vacations are much more fun when your children know something about their destination. If you are going to a famous place or city, read about it to your children. Let them keep a journal of what they see and experience. They can also draw maps of places they've visited.

Exposes a Child to New Information 89

A toddler's world is largely confined to pre-school and home. Books open a child's mind to libraries filled with stories about new things. . . new cultures. . . and the universe.

90 Encourages Good Judgment

Judgment is taught through many instances of 'What if.' When we engage our children's minds through reading, we encourage them to recognize what they need to know to make good judgments.

Helps Create a Positive Lifestyle 91

Our daily activity is a life-long lesson. All we do becomes part of the fabric of our children's lives, as well as things we don't do. Our conscious choice to spend quality time with our children will have a positive effect on our lives and theirs.

92 Helps Children Mature

By reading to our children, we expose them to life's experiences. This helps a child understand life's occurrences and helps them mature.

Encourages Positive Attitudes 93

Your positive, helpful behavior is communicated to your child when reading to them. The child feels loved and worthy of your attention.

94 Encourages Healthy Compromises

Compromise is not the same as giving in, or just being nice. Healthy compromise is achieved when all people involved in the issue have been heard, valued and considered. Our conversations with our children during shared reading time often addresses the issues common to them.

Teaches the Meaning of Commitment 95

When our children see our commitment to them through reading every day, they will be more likely to commit themselves to family and personal goals from a young age.

96 Helps Prepare Them for Life's Challenges

Reading about life's situations in books can give our children the safe distance needed to ask the questions that are on their minds. By spending quality time with them, we can offer guidance, explanations and suggestions while allowing them to think and make judgments. Through this exchange, they develop a better understanding of life.

Trains Them to Speak Clearly 97

Often times, we must pay close attention to what our children are trying to say. While their vocabulary may be limited, their feelings and ideas are vast. As we read to them, we are training them to speak more clearly... and training ourselves to hear their messages.

98 Teaches the Relationship between Letters & Words

While reading, you can teach your young child to spell a few special words, such as his or her name... stop or go. By drawing attention to these frequently occurring words, the child begins to understand how letters form words.

Teaches the Appreciation of Life 99

We are surrounded by the everyday miracles and mysteries of life. The more we try to understand mysteries, like the mystery of birth, the more conscious we become of our roles in the world. Through reading our children can learn about life's many mysteries.

100

Teaches Tolerance

By taking time to patiently read to our children, we are teaching patience and tolerance.

Teaches Leadership

101

The skills to be a leader are varied. But a primary factor in leadership is the ability to interact with others while expressing and listening to many points-of-view to reach a goal. Children do not become leaders overnight. Reading about other leaders helps them realize that they need time to mature and that they'll make mistakes. In short, children need involved parents to help them gain knowledge, use it, assess it and form a life plan that will help ensure their personal and public success.

Appendix

SUGGESTED READING
For
Toddlers

Blackstone, Stella	Baby High, Baby Low
Brown, Margaret Wise	Little Donkey Close Your Eyes
Cabban, Vanessa	Bertie and Small and the Brave Sea Journey
Cabrera, Jane	Panda Big and Panda Small
Chorao, Kay	Knock At the Door and Other Baby Action Rhymes
Dale, Penny	Ten Play Hide-and-Seek
Ford, Miela	Mom and Me
Haynes, Max	Ticklemonster and Me
Hill, Eric	Spot Sleeps Over
Hindley, Judy	Eyes, Nose, Fingers and Toes
Hiskey, Iris	I Like a Snack On an Iceberg
Kopper, Lisa	Daisy Knows Best
Lawrence, Michael	Baby Loves
Lebrun, Claude	Little Brown Bear Is Growing Up
McDonnell, Flora	Splash!
Miller, Margaret	Big and Little
Miranda, Anne	Beep! Beep!
Morton, Christine	Picnic Farm
Murphy, Mary	Caterpillar's Wish
Newcome, Zita	Animal Fun
Oxenbury, Helen	Tom and Pippo and the Bicycle
Rogers, Alan	Green Bear
Simon, Francesca	Calling All Toddlers
Siomades, Lorianne	Itsy Bitsy Spider
Tafuri, Nancy	Have You Seen My Duckling?
Waddell, Martin	Owl Babies
Winter, Susan	Me Too
Young, Ruth	Golden Bear

Bibliographies compiled by System Youth Services of the Palm Beach County Library System.

SUGGESTED READING
For
Beginning Readers

Avi	Abigail Takes the Wheel
Baker, Barbara	One Saturday Afternoon
Bechtold, Lisze	Buster, the Very Shy Dog
Bernstein, Margery	That Cat!
Capucilli, Alyssa	Happy Birthday, Biscuit!
Cazet, Denys	Minnie and Moo Go to the Moon
Cosby, Bill	One Dark and Scary Night
Dodds, Dayle Ann	Ghost and Pete
Eastman, P. D.	Best Nest
Edwards, Frank	Is the Spaghetti Ready?
Farber, Erica	Ooey Gooey
Finch, Margo	Lunch Bunch
Hoban, Lillian	Arthur's Birthday Party
Jensen, Patsy	Loose-Tooth Luke
Leonard, Marcia	Dress-Up
Lobel, Arnold	Owl At Home
Low, Alice	Witch Who Was Afraid Of Witches
McKay, Sindy	Jack and the Beanstalk
Maestro, Marco	Geese Find the Missing Piece
Meister, Cari	When Tiny Was Tiny
Miles, Betty	Sky Is Falling
Minarik, Else	No Fighting, No Biting!
Moncure, Jane	Dragon In a Wagon
Morris, Kimberly	Molly In the Middle
Rylant, Cynthia	Poppleton in Fall
Sathre, Vivian	Slender Ella and Her Fairy Hogfather
Schreiber, Anne	Shoes, Shoes, Shoes
Seuss, Dr.	There's A Wocket In My Pocket!
Simon, Charnan	Mud!
Wallace, Karen	Duckling Days
Weston, Martha	Cats Are Like That

Bibliographies compiled by System Youth Services of the Palm Beach County Library System.

SUGGESTED READING
For
Pre K - Kindergarten

Alborough, Jez	My Friend Bear
Antoine, Heloise	Curious Kids Go to Preschool
Asch, Frank	Baby Bird's First Nest
Carlstrom, Nancy	What a Scare, Jesse Bear
Gomi, Taro	Crocodile and the Dentist
Harrison, Joanna	When Mom Turned Into a Monster
Hoberman, Mary Ann	Miss Mary Mack
Hutchins, Pat	It's My Birthday!
Kroninger, Stephen	If I Crossed the Road
Layton, Neal	Smile If You're Human
McGeorge, Constance	Boomer's Big Surprise
Monks, Lydia	Cat Barked?
Mazer, Anne	Fixits
Miranda, Anne	To Market, To Market
Rathmann, Peggy	10 Minutes Till Bedtime
Shannon, David	David Goes to School
Sloat, Teri	Farmer Brown Goes Round and Round
Steig, William	Pete's A Pizza
Stuve-Bodeen, Stephanie	Elizabeti's Doll
Waddell, Martin	Good Job, Little Bear
Walters, Catherine	When Will It Be Spring?
Whybrow, Ian	Sammy and the Dinosaurs
Wells, Rosemary	Yoko
Vagin, Vladimir	Enormous Carrot
Ziefert, Harriet	Pushkin Meets the Bundle

Bibliographies compiled by System Youth Services of the Palm Beach County Library System.

SUGGESTED READING
For
Grades 1-3

Anholt, Laurence	Summerhouse
Armour, Peter	Stop That Pickle!
Bloom, Becky	Wolf!
Borden, Louise	Good Luck, Mrs. K!
Brown, Marc	Locked in the Library!
Bunting, Eve	So Far From the Sea
Cocca-Leffler, Maryann	Mr. Tanen's Ties
David, Lawrence	Beetle Boy
Duffey, Betsy	Cody's Secret Admirer
Ernst, Lisa Campbell	Stella Louella's Runaway Book
Foster, Joanna	Magpies' Nest
Fox, Mem	Whoever You Are
Giff, Patricia	Glass Slipper For Rosie
Gonzalez, Lucia	Bossy Gallito
Havill, Juanita	Jamaica and the Substitute Teacher
Joyce, Susan	ABC Animal Riddles
Joyce, William	Buddy
Ketteman, Helen	Bubba the Cowboy Prince
Kirk, David	Nova's Ark
Kline, Suzy	Song Lee and the "I Hate You" Notes
Lorbiecki, Marybeth	Sister Anne's Hands
Marshall, James	Cut-Ups Crack Up
Polacco, Patricia	Mrs. Mack
Sansone, Adele	Little Green Goose
Tusa, Tricia	Bunnies In My Head
Van Allsburg, Chris	Sweetest Fig
Warner, Sally	Private Lily

Bibliographies compiled by System Youth Services of the Palm Beach County Library System.

SUGGESTED READING
For
Grades 4-5

Alexander, Lloyd	Gypsy Rizka
Burnett, Frances Hodgson	Little Princess
Danziger, Paula	Amber Brown Is Feeling Blue
Calmenson, Stephanie	Rockin' Reptiles
Cleary, Beverly	Ramona's World
Erdrich, Louise	Birchbark House
Gantos, Jack	Joey Pigza Swallowed the Key
Gorman, Carol	Miraculous Makeover of Lizard Flanagan
Gregory, Kristiana	Great Railroad Race : The Diary of Libby West
Kehret, Peg	I'm Not Who You Think I Am
Keller, Holly	Angela's Top-Secret Computer Club
Haddix, Margaret	Among the Hidden
Hesse, Karen	Music of Dolphins
Johnson, Angela	Heaven
Lawrence, Iain	Wreckers
Levine, Gail	Ella Enchanted
Mahy, Margaret	Horribly Haunted School
McKean, Thomas	My Evil Twin
Moss, Marissa	Amelia Takes Command
Naylor, Phyllis Reynolds	Boys Start the War
Nixon, Joan Lowery	Aggie's Home
Osborne, Mary Pope	Standing In the Light
Peck, Richard	Long Way From Chicago
Pullman, Philip	Clockwork : Or All Wound Up
Rowling, J.K	Harry Potter and the Sorcerer's Stone
Sachar, Louis	Wayside School Is Falling Down
Wisler, G. Clifton	Caleb's Choice

Bibliographies compiled by System Youth Services of the Palm Beach County Library System.

SUGGESTED READING
For
Young Adults

Cooney, Caroline B.	Driver's Ed
Cushman, Karen	Catherine, Called Birdy
Ferris, Jean	Bad
Griffin, Adele	Other Sheperds
Grimes, Nikki	Jazmin's Notebook
Hesser, Terry Spencer	Kissing Doorknobs
Hobbs, Will	Far North
Howe, Norma	Adventures of Blue Avenger
Jordan, Sherryl	Raging Quiet
Keller, Beverly	Amazon Papers
Koertge, Ronald	Harmony Arms
Littke, Lael	Haunted Sister
Metzger, Lois	Missing Girls
Mikaelsen, Ben	Petey
Myers, Walter Dean	Journal of Scott Pendleton Collins
Napoli, Donna Jo	For the Love Of Venice
Naylor, Phyllis Reynolds	Alice On the Outside
Nixon, Joan Lowery	Haunting
Paulsen, Gary	Soldier's Heart
Peck, Robert Newton	Nine Man Tree
Prince, Maggie	House On Hound Hill
Qualey, Marsha	Thin Ice
Rubin, Susan	Emily In Love
Rubinstein, Gillian	Beyond the Labyrinth
Temple, Frances	Ramsay Scallop
Watkins, Yoko Kawashima	My Brother, My Sister, and I
Werlin, Nancy	Killer's Cousin
Williams, Carol Lynch	My Angelica
Yolen, Jane	Armageddon Summer
Zindel, Paul	Raptor

Bibliographies compiled by System Youth Services of the Palm Beach County Library System.

SUGGESTED READING
For
Parents and Teachers

"Read All About It! Great Read-Aloud Stories, Poems and Newspaper Pieces for Preteens and Teens." A collection of 50 pieces ranging from poems ("Casey at the Bat") to short stories.

"Read to Me: Raising Kids who love to Read"
By Bernice E. Cullinan.

"Kick The TV Habit," by Steve and Ruth Bennett.
A family handbook for handling and controlling television watching by young children.

The Cooperative Children's Book Center at the University of Wisconsin: "CCBC Choices." A guide to the year's best in children's literature. Write to them for the latest price of the guide. CCBC, 4290 Helen C. White Hall, 600 N. Park St., Madison, WI 53706.

"Children's Books of the Year." An annotated listing of 600 books. Published by the Child Study Children's Book Committee at Bank Street College, 610 W. 112th St., New York, N.Y. 10025

"The Shelter of Each Other: Rebuilding our Families," by Pipher.

"The Book of Virtues," by William Bennett. A conservative look at the role of morality in modern-day society.

"50 SimpleThings You Can Do to Raise a Child Who Loves to Read," by Kathy Zahler, Arco Press.

"Teach a Child to Read with Children's Books," by Mark Thogmartin, Ed Info Press.

Resource Guide

Reading is Fundamental
877-RIF-READ

Pizza Hut's Book It! Program
P.O. Box 2999, Wichita, KS 67201

National Center for Family Literacy
325 West Main Street, Suite 200
Louisville, KY 40202-4251

Future Editions

Become one of our writers...

- Star Group International is planning the second edition to this book called, *101 Plus Reasons to READ to Your Child*. We invite all our readers to submit their reasons to read for this edition.

- Name recognition will be given to contributors whose reasons are published.

- To submit your reasons to read send them to:

---

101 Plus Reasons to READ to Your Child

Star Group International, Inc.
777 S. Flagler Drive
8th Floor, West Tower
West Palm Beach, FL 33401

Or fax your reasons to:
(561) 586-7928

Children... Tell us why you love to read

- Star Group International is planning another book called *101 Reasons CHILDREN Love to Read*. We invite all of you to submit your Reasons to Read.

- Name recognition will be given to contributors whose reasons are published.

- To submit your reasons to read send them to:

About the Author

Brenda Star knows first-hand that reading is an essential element of a family unit... generating communication, understanding and unity. Having read to her two children and grandchildren, Brenda's love for books and reading eventually led her to become an author and publisher.

Brenda appreciates the importance of reading and writing. Reflecting on her life as a working mother, she realized that reading aloud to her children established a lifetime bond with them that is the foundation of their relationship today. Brenda wants to encourage others to share this experience with their children. That is why she published *101 Reasons to READ to Your Child*.

Brenda Star is the founder of Star Group International, a book publishing, public relations and marketing firm.

Star Group International, Inc.

S tar Group International was established to help individuals and companies expand their reputation and enhance their credibility throughout the community or throughout the world.

Over a hundred seasoned professionals, many of whom are national leaders in their fields, make up the foundation of Star Group International's expertise in marketing & advertising, public relations, book publishing, and image enhancement. Having this full range of resources available under a single corporate structure offers integrated accountability in marketing strategy, work product and follow-through.

By developing local, regional, national and international marketing campaigns, Star Group helps corporations, businesses, industries and other professionals send their message to their target audience.

For additional information contact:

Star Group International, Inc.
777 S. Flagler Drive, West Tower, 8th Floor
West Palm Beach, FL 33401
(561) 547-0667
fax (561) 586-7928
info hotline (561) 616-6328
www.stargroup.net

Dan Young

Dan Young is a staunch supporter of the ideals set forth by Northwood University and its founder Dr. Arthur E. Turner, and it was in part, through his generosity, that this book was made possible.

Dan Young was introduced to the business world over forty years ago. Over the years, he has owned several diverse businesses in multiple states. Today an honorable and successful businessman, Dan continues to focus on new business development while splitting his time between his homes in Indiana and Florida.

Dan shows a keen interest in providing opportunities for young people with initiative to reach their potential. It is because of his interest in today's youth that he supported Northwood University and Star Group International in publishing this book.

Northwood University

Northwood University is a professional school of management offering bachelor and associate degrees in 13 different business and management disciplines. Celebrating 40 years of higher education, Northwood was founded in 1959 by Dr. Arthur Turner and Dr. Gary Stauffer who believed that colleges were not preparing students with the type of management skills and training necessary to compete in the ever-changing economy. Since, the University has grown to 12,000 students systemwide.

The Florida campus, situated upon 83 acres in West Palm Beach, boasts modern and attractive facilities, small classrooms, a 20:1 student-faculty ratio, and a commitment to providing students with an outstanding faculty who have had real-world experience within their academic disciplines.

Northwood's Florida campus currently enrolls some 1,000 students from 28 states and 32 different countries. The university's intercollegiate athletic program combined with numerous clubs and activities supplements the academic program and creates a truly balanced education preparing students for the demands of an everchanging world.

For further information contact:

Office of Admissions
Northwood University
2600 N. Military Trail
West Palm Beach, FL 33409
(561) 478-5500   (800) 458-8325
website: http://www.northwood.edu